bonehouse

bonehouse

Erika Brumett

*For my friend Lisa,
with admiration & appreciation.
Best,
Erika*

Green Linden Press

bonehouse
Copyright © 2018, Erika Brumett
All rights reserved.

First Printing, 2018

ISBN: 978-0-9992263-2-2

Design: Christopher Nelson
Cover Art: *Botanical Cabeça* by Diego Max

Green Linden Press
208 Broad Street South
Grinnell, IA 50112

www.greenlindenpress.com

A portion of proceeds supports reforestation efforts.
Printed on recycled paper.

Contents

Worms	1
Passage	3
Three Men Playing Poker Post-Mortem	4
Appendix Ode	6
The Longing of Anatomical Drawings	7
Cunnilingus	8
To Name Is to Own	10
"Biologist Documents Creative Act of Dolphin Masturbation"	11
Where They Love	13
Rewriting a Greeting Card	14
Revenants	15
What My Father Couldn't Answer	16
Bulletin from the Living	18
Panties Left in a Cemetery	19
Hyperkulturemia	20
"Artist Bioengineers Van Gogh's Ear. It's Alive ... and It Can Hear You!"	21
Lithopedion	23
Learning What Two-Year-Olds Know	24
View From My Father's Room	25
Rabbit's Foot	26
Random Attack Caught on Camera	27
Spontaneous Human Combustion	29
Visit to the Phrenologist	30
Cleaning Out My Father's Closet	32
Untitled, Acrylic on Canvas, by Rani (Asian Elephant, Age 30)	34
Animals in Outer Space	35
Aubade for a Dead Lover	37

Terminal Velocity	39
Acknowledgments	40
About the Poet	41

bonehouse

    noun, from Old English, *bānhūs*:
    1) the living body, the chest, the breast.
    2) an ossuary, a structure for holding the dead.

Worms

"It may be doubted whether there is any other animal which has played so important a part in the history of the world, as have these lowly, organized beings." —Charles Darwin

Little tillers. Ploughs of night-
 writhe and gizzard. Eyeless, they grind
  through hummus—through leaf tip, rock
bit, rootlet—burrowing tubal
 as the tubes they burrow. Dirt-
  serpents, vermicelli, bait. Hook-
   clowns, inchlings, doll snakes. Sectioned,
  intestinal—each a squiggle
of innard—a stretch of entrail
or colon. *Intelligent, unsung*

creatures, Darwin noted, *humble men*
 born blind and dumb. He kept some
  in the cellar, let a few loose
   in the drawing room, where he used
    his son's bassoon to test their sense
   of sound. (Low flats, blown long, made them twine
with squirm.) Outside, Charles tossed cinders
 on lime, charred marl on ashes, watched
  as earth swallowed earth by way of worm-
   work. As all was churned, pulled down. Stone-

  henge rose from snow *like stacked bones*
 that winter, when Darwin knelt—
in his final year—in its circle's center.
When he bent his beard over a slab
 of fallen sarsen, sunken under worm
  cast and loam that had frozen.
   To know them before going below

to join them. Their ganglions and five hearts.
Their slow, slow force—aerating,
burying—alive with decay.

Passage

—Audio art installation (underground walkway to University of Washington Medical Center)

Were they jays? Swallows, or finches? Dark-eyed
juncos, robins maybe? Hitchcockian—
that walk to ICU—through the tunnel

of birds—toward my father's room. There were flocks
and flocks. Hundreds, thousands, hundreds of thousands
of verdins, or larks, or starlings—all calling,

calling—stuck deep down below hospital
grounds. What artist thought that cacophony
might comfort? The soundtrack whistled on-

loop, on and on—siskins or kinglets—singing,
singing raucous at once, dawn until dusk
until dawn. Notes echoed off walls as one,

shrill song. A trillion violins, strings
pulled thin, then plucked by icepicks. The carcass-
hymn of bones hollowed by wind, a tune with air

for marrow. And on certain visits, whippoorwills
or wrens—chickadees, pipits, or sparrows—
could only have been banshees, keen after

keen, screaming. The passage shuddered, rang.
There, space narrowed. Shrank beneath sound's weight.
Canaries were once carried through shafts such as that,

their hush forewarning. But under floors, wards, and breath
cut short, the birds kept chirping. Flights above,
I still heard them. In his room, silence sang.

Three Men Playing Poker Post-Mortem

—Displayed at the Bodies exhibit (a gallery of preserved cadavers)

Propped around a felt-top table,
                  three of a kind, dealt in behind
red museum rope. They've been scalped
                  to skulls, skinned for exhibition,
a marvel of muscle and bone.
                  Curators and plastination
set them here. Here where the game's gone
                  guts-to-open, Texas Hold'em,
where one man tilts his cranium,
                  stares sockets at the pot, at live bets
just thrown down. All antes are up.
                  It's tough to tell who's bluffing now.

Or what thoughts once shuffled, riffled
                  then flipped. What hands each man once held
close, fanned out with hope, then folded.
                  But who these bodies were matters
little this round. Nothing's at stake.
                  Embalmers faked each poker face,
so the dealer slumps with a straight.
                  The corpse to his right white-knuckles
jacks. Posing fleshless, he passes
                  aces, sneaks them beneath the rack.

This could be Vegas—The Oasis—
                  its gilt and cold glitz. Or maybe
some basement men's night, wives upstairs,
                  gin-bitching in the kitchenette.
Tendons glisten under halogen,
                  and the third stiff sits at a pitch,
leans scapula in as if to ask

               how the deck went cold, and who called
the clock. Why spotlights slice through him
                     like luck—slanting past the slats of his ribs.

Appendix Ode

The organ looks much like a geoduck, all cock-
limp and tubal. Labeled useless, vestigial,
it crimps above the right hip. Evolutionary
baggage, this sac was once thought. A throwback
to when man foraged scabland, digesting the wood-
scrape of roots, gnawed on raw mastodon in cave

nooks. Poor vesicle, toxic and scalpeled. So long
catalogued with the coccyx, tonsils, and the male
nipple. So frequently assessed as the bowel's tag-
along pest, as the intestines' overstayed houseguest.
From middle French, "to hang upon," its name
suggests an excess of flesh, or some manuscript's

expendable addendum. But our *processus
vermiformis* is far from pointless. Pressed against
the cecum, its basin creates a haven
for bacteria—a dangling garden—bursting buds
of good gut flora. That kid with the spade-
shaped wound, his immune system will never

rebloom. Da Vinci first drew one—a doodle, less
sketch than lampoon, cartoonish in shrivel—scribbled,
appendix vermix: little worm affixed. Indeed,
what grit. Through storms of germs and surgical snips,
centuries of scorn and biological shifts, it stays
true, persists. Praise this—at last—the septic, the steadfast.

The Longing of Anatomical Drawings

—A diagram of reproductive systems

Male. Female. A pastel couple, cleaved
down the middle. They've been halved,
    pear-perfect, navel to kneecap.
        Sliced clean, the duo wears nothing
but labels: bladder, seminal
vesicle, labia. She is contained.
    All corpuscle, yolk, potential—
        coiled becoming. Beside her, in side-
view he grows beyond himself.
Bulb-heavy. Bulge of root, tuber, burl.
    It's difficult to feel romantic
    in a clinic—butcher paper bed
sheet, stirrups spread eager, a bouquet
of swabs. But there's a tenderness
    to this pair, to their hopeless
    and headless abstinence.
Perhaps it's the nearness of his sketch
to hers. Poised mid-approach, forever
    out of touch, always one thrust away.
        Above steel trays, they pose flayed, on display,
separated by the abyss of an inch.
This is a long-distance relationship,
    a love of lack, of want-but-cannot-
    have. Together each aches alone, severed,

pining. And what could be more satisfying?

Cunnilingus

The word sounds like a low-hung cloud,
    weighed down below scuds of cirrus.

Yet its vowels lift—softer, loftier,
    than cumulus. Cunnilingus

could be the name of some Roman
    emperor. Or a butterfly's

phase, that stage of glisten and change,
    when silk glands lace the chrysalis.

Cunnilingus could be a cyst
    on the esophagus, the pause

before a lie, a fantasy
    novel's protagonist pegasus.

Its syllables flit the tongue, gill-slit
    the lips, as might the secret

dialects of sly, benthic fish.
    The suffix, in fact, means "to lick."

Its prefix, predictably, is vulvic.
    But why did cunnilingus slip

from diction, only to be forgotten
    with the argot of Victorian

porn and couch-fainting vixens?
    Imagine cunnilingus high-

fived over pitchers of Budweiser,
    sexted on iPhones, murmured in bed-

rooms, where night churns and little matters
    but the waves, the swell, the way

moonglow makes blankets look liquid.
    What term better enacts subject?

It ticks across the palate, whorls
    around the uvula, lapping

sound toward meaning. The word
    is origami—folding,

unfolding—paper too moist
    to hold the V-creases of cranes.

Cunnilingus opens one mouth—splits
    it slick—so as to open another.

To Name Is to Own

*"It is permissible to name things discovered by me,
thus it shall be: the love or sweetness of Venus."*
—*Anatomist, Matteo Renaldo Colombo (upon discovering the clitoris)*

But what of the days before brave Colombo,
   before he rambled off solo, wander-
lusted over mounds soft as moss?
   Did Venus even see it, this genus-
less fish, spume-slick from the foam she rode in on?

Button or pearl, nubbin or bean. Sudden anemone,
   bud of the sea. Goblin or nut, chickpea
or seed—in Germany, it's called, *kitzler,*
   which translates to "tickler." Yet cuter still,
the Greek diminutive, *keitys*: a derivative

of "miniature hill." Slug or bulb,
   little chub or diddler. The clitoris exists
in ostriches, it stretches eight inches,
   and kangaroos: they have two. Acorn or worm,
grundle horn or twaddler. A half-nibbled plum,

left in sun and brine wind. Munchlet or glan,
   hood-monk or scrunchling—a caboodle
of nerves—8,000 receptors plumping. The organ
   may be, to many, quite foreign. Or something kept,
a treacherous pet, approached with shameful watchfulness.

Owned but ignored, possessed yet dismissed—
   what would Venus think of this? Maybe she'd rather not
have washed up, bashful on a half-shell, opted
   instead to stay at sea. To cache away
her curled snail, crimped as kelp in its tide bed.

"Biologist Documents Creative Act of Dolphin Masturbation"

—International Journal of Aquatic Science

What did sight sound like, click-
    clicking off coral? And how did sound
        look, echoed back from the mouths
  of alcoves?   *dolphin arousal*
noted during sonar (rapid pulse
    tones   dorsal stiffening   engorged
        genital slit)   object of interest
    quickly located   Were boat hulls cloud-
drift, the sky full and bright with star-
    fish, was it romantic?   *eel fight/*
        flight instincts malfunctioned
    So once hooked, the eel stayed put, slick-
wriggling this dolphin's penis?
    biological motivations remain
        unclear   Is want a wet rhythm—
varied as waves—is lust just water,
brine surging through veins?   *cetacean*
    phalli retract into membrane
        flaps on the belly   coiling
    uncoiling   with constant   urgent   erection
Then, in a sense, two sea serpents
    met, each at hunt but hidden?
        the anguilliform's larval gut
    was of the filamentous subset
facilitating a prehensile slide
    hence stimulation for the subject
        (see illustration)   Did squid look on—
    ogle-eyed—beside prawn and the red-open
lips of anemones? What happened

next, what did they do when it was all done?
cetacean completion achieved
in seconds   Will the eel recall
that throb under-gill, his mirrored
form's shiver?   *pleasure in the primitive
limbic system   imprints forever*

Where They Love

On carpets, lawns, staircases twisting
to strangers' apartments. In cars, clawed tubs,
the darkest of gardens. Once at thirty-
thousand feet, the horizon slit scarlet.
    But the closet's their favorite. Its interior
    is mirrored—folding eight doors at angles—
    redoubling their coupling again and again,
    reflecting reflections in infinite regression.
When she licks the length of him, ten women
bend, then ten behind them, mouths open in tandem.
When he arches, charges back where he became,
a hundred men bray, pull her hair like a mane.
    This walk-in's packed, cramped standing-room-only.
    It's an orgy (but reversed, and a lot less work).
    Bodies collide, divide, kaleidoscope walls,
    all enthralled to be both watcher and watched.
Above him, she's rapt, casting fractals
like shadows. Smaller, smaller still, they circle
themselves—locking, gawking at their own looking—
awed slick by this glimpse at omniscience.

Rewriting a Greeting Card

*"You'll be the first thought when I rise,
The last thought when I close my eyes."*
        —*Hallmark*™

Yet there's a persistence to the meaning-
less. To the routine, the tedious,
the insignificant. What if that last thought
to flash from synapse to synapse—arcing
electric from nerve path to nerve path—what if
the final image to imprint like sun
shaft on the back of lids closed old and world-
done and thin, what if that thought's not of you,

Love? But of the humdrum. A man on a bus,
glimpsed just once, from a street, in a dream
where the plot got lost as sleep wore off. Or stars.
Maybe I'll watch only blotches of light
clots at white-out, a stand-up-too-fast-head-rush.
Could be jump rope rhymes, jingles. One of those late-night
infomercials—*call now, we don't have much time
left, there's so little time.* Or some dumb sitcom's theme song.

It's been said, that last thoughts last for the rest
of ever. That reflections at the second
of death extend and extend in a never-
ending on-and-on. A whole lot's been said
though, Love. Should just the absurd endure,
the mundane transcend—strangers' laughter, dawn
the texture of a worn bedspread—may you come
in the banal to me then: in their silence after,

and in light—in that same, threadbare light—yet again.

Revenants

Was it Freud who said dead parents always
stand, hand in hand, at the edge of your bed
during sex? Maybe he meant this statement
metaphorically. And yet, there they are

again. Silent. Twilit by the dim
you let in so as to see the salt-glint
sweat gleams on skin. But just when you begin
to tongue each inch—then plunge, surge, plunge toward bliss—

there's Dad, in that plaid bathrobe Mom monogrammed
upside-down. And here she is. Your mother, haloed
by hair curlers, wearing her balding fur
slippers, her stare that says, "Oh no. Oh, Hon,

don't." Maybe it's the way Dad stoops over.
How robe folds droop open—just so—to show
ribs, clavicle: the scythe-curve of bone.
Or perhaps it's the quiver of Mom's upper lip,

the pinch of her cringe under cold cream, which stops
all lust mid-thrusting. Just what was Freud suggesting?
Why must their figures, hunched against dusk
and each other, insist on a visit at times

such as this? Sigmund might have seen them—less
as pests, or incestuous threats—more as embodiments
of intimacy. Its circularity.
Consider your mother. See how she blinks

wrinkles? And look, there are stars. Galaxies
of hot flecks the hall lamp dots on Dad's specs.
Side by side, your parents spark loss across want.
As dark parts and you arch. Aching with light.

What My Father Couldn't Answer

"Patients with bulbar ALS may very well regret—though stripped of the ability to speak, trapped beyond family reach—their decision to extend life on a ventilator machine. Yet how would we ever know?"
—*Tough Choices: Facing Lough Gehrig's Disease,*
  Pacific Regional Medical Journal

was it worth it   all the nurses
and the wordlessness   swabs   trach prods
neck gauze puffed as a goddamn ruff
was it worth your while to have stayed
with us   were we enough   enough
just to watch grow up   then grow soft
softening   even as you hardened
stiff under tubes on that living
room bed   entombed   as if Pompeiian
locked rigid in your own long limbs
about which   I often wondered
did they ache   or itch till they ached
but you couldn't say   isn't bulbar
a vulgar term   and how did it churn
around your mouth when no sound
would come out   like a slow cud chew
on mud   or closer to shame   its bile
sour panic taste that makes the jaw
clamp down   remember the mare
you told me about   that brown bay
on your great grandpa's lot   the one
who tossed you at a dumb plod walk
wrung your throat where the clothesline ran taut
what was her name   old sue   maude   kate
would you have thought it odd   some late nights
I wake up   sheet twisted gut rot sick
because I can't recall   were you afraid

were you proud of who we became
was dusk's blue slide the rolling back
of eyes   and did you know your last breath
your last breath   dad   it was a sigh

Bulletin from the Living

Not sure if you've heard—this place melts, it burns—
    never been hotter, dear. They say glaciers
        will thaw to water then swallow us all.
            Waves already lapped up that gap-plank pier.
But autumn still mottles my window. Frost
    blurs morning, blots out sky with whorls of rime.
        Since you left: our dive bar closed, beards are back
            in vogue, and Burma's not Burma,
it's Myanmar now. Also of note:
    Pluto got demoted, that bedpost
        we broke—I glued it—and everyone's
            genome is charted, like some new-found coast
of Atlantis. Perhaps of interest:
    no more floppy disks, home phones, or love
        notes on coasters. No more white rhinos, either.
            You should know: Updike, Marquez, Sendak—gone.
Last week, a man in a lab made his own star.
    We've learned now how to manipulate
        the memories of mice, and some sort of rocket
            landed on some kind of comet. Your mom
died. Ever wonder why we all want
    god? A man in a lab figured that out, too.
        Not much has happened: there've been turf wars,
            famines, cities on fire. Lover, the other
night I saw you, dim-lit, out my window—
    expressionless and crowd-pressed against dusk
        and a bus stop. I put my hand to the glass, to the ice
            on the pane. I pulled the shade on your shadow.

Panties Left in a Cemetery

Their fabric is latticed, delicate,
    crotch-to-the-sky beside a grave.
Twisted waistband. Little satin bow.
    The threading webs, red in sunshaft,
mauve in the shade of the stone.

Someone loved here. Moaned below oaks,
    groped above bones. Who lifted hips,
tasted lace, dropped soft cloth on clover?
    Did light sift, moths flit, teeth pluck elastic?
Maybe mourners coupled, thrusted through grief.

Or did kids ditch math class, come
    lusting down dew paths, find this patch?
Stillness, tall grass, fountains crying lichen.
    Just children, eagerlings fingering
bottle caps, loss, bra straps.

At a glance, the undies are a doily,
    a hankie from a wake. Wadded,
forgotten, they rot where crosses
    moss and cherubs watch. Where daisies
lie flat, crushed by small deaths.

Hyperkulturemia

—Also known as Stendhal Syndrome, a disputed disorder said to cause tachycardia, fainting, confusion—even hallucinations—when subjects are exposed to works of art.

Reeling below ceiling frescos,
Stendhal wrote how vertigo whirled
the basilica—how he knelt,
wept, palmed along walls—while soprano
angels echoed, while a terror
of cherubim gyred the dome high

over him. Some said omen. Claimed
he'd been chosen. Others thought—awe-
sick, panicked—Stendhal was hyper-
susceptible to an aesthetic blitz—
to Stabat Mater on plaster—psycho-
somatic fits of fear and bliss.

Regardless, psychiatrists insist
this syndrome doesn't exist. Dismissed:
that tourist who stripped, hucked a gift-
shop teacup at the *Mona Lisa*; also
one who slow-licked a Christ's cold, stone
lips; then the man who broke his fist (sucker-

punched *Manneken Pis*). Were Neanderthals
such madmen as this? Maybe—enthralled
as Stendhal—they crawled after bison
who outloped charcoal. Could be
hand prints signaled from cave walls.
And perhaps—rapt—they waved back.

"Artist Bioengineers Van Gogh's Ear. It's Alive ... and It Can Hear You!"

> —*Advertisement for a museum exhibit, featuring a functioning auditory system made from pig guts, synthetic material, and the DNA of Theo's great-grandson.*

Vincent pressed a parcel once
into the hands of a whore. *Dearest,
guard this object most carefully,*

he told her, as its bow wicked ochre-
brown and dripped, as she stared down
at his blood on the ground. And now,

suspended in transparent gel,
set behind glass and valves and vents:
a live replica. Organelles

reorganized. From cartilage
to centrifuge, tissue sample
to pipette: an appendage

which was never appended.
An idol no disciple ever
severed. The ear appears

withered—pale in reliquary—
where gallery-goers whisper secrets,
fears, wishes through small speakers,

into the organ's open atrium.
Their syllables spiral around
and around the auricle, inward

toward drum membrane, past ossicles,
thrumming at last on the cochlea.
And as for Vincent? What would he have made

of this, all gauzed and lost outside
the brothel? Could some trace of him
be tuning-in from ersatz skin?

Maybe—alone, at such distance—Vincent
just listens to the cross-hatch scrape
of static. Bristles scritch-scratching.

LITHOPEDION

*—Greek for "rock child": a fetus that grows outside of the uterus,
where it calcifies into a solid, mineral-like concretion.*

    Stone cherub, chipped from schist, curled in the crypt
of its mother's ribs. Pitted. Twisted.
    A babe made of bedrock, with granite cries
        and pyrite for eyebrights. Archeologists
    lifted the first—solidified, encysted,
        the size of a fist—from a dig site
in Damascus, dating conception to Stone
Age days. Noting a likeness to igneous.
    Or to a castle's little gargoyle,
        split from turret and mortar. A creature
    fit for some marble-fawned garden, where fountains
        spout moss and statues crumble in night mist.
    Where darkness encases. Cauls an unborn's shock
of calcite locks, the spine bent fetal, moonglint
    off its single tooth. Sculptors once thought
        that shape lay latent in rock. Waiting. Gestating.
    Patient for chisel or riffler. Yet form
        might get pent up—locked in—where being begins.
    There, its yolk sac is a crust of shale,
brittle as snailshell, at which the child kicks
    and kicks, suckling dust through rock cracks.

Learning What Two-Year-Olds Know

"Childhood is the kingdom where nobody dies."
—Edna St. Vincent Millay

Under dusk and alders, catkins husked
    by autumn wind, my stepkid kills ants.
        She's exacting in her attack,
merciless in galoshes, stalking
    their dirt bunker with a stick. I watch her
        untangle salal with its tip, poke soil,
till ants spill black and lacquer-backed
    all over their hill. Her boot hovers—rubber
        sole ready—above loam, deadfall, small lives
running on rot. *Oh no, poor ant*, she cries,
    before crushing one after another—then one
        more—into ocher leaves, or some insect
hereafter. *Poor, ant*. Stomp. *Ohhh, ant*. Stamp.
    There are twigs in her pigtails, thrushes hushed
        together for nightfall, so I lift her
from her slaughter, my brand-new daughter,
    this hellion in rain boots and a snicker,
        hold her—as if she didn't know better—rock-
rock her the whole walk home.

View From My Father's Room

"When nerve cells wither, patients may lose the ability to speak ... also suffering from the paradoxical condition of muscle softening, as the spinal cord hardens."
—Understanding ALS, Lander-Salter Medical Journal

It's been some time since we've seen sky—
                    the pine grows over the window
now. Tangle of gnarl, spindle limb,
                    needles stitching in. Branches stretch.
Neurons curl. His jaw just unlatched
                    again. The mandible dangles,
open at an angle, yawned off-hinge.
                    I fumble under rubber tubes,
pumps that shunt, nudge the chair on wheels,
                    plunge both thumbs toward tongue and gum.
His mouth lolls, makes an O to swallow
                    all we won't get back. Twigs say,
scritch. Dusk says, *hush*. He can't say
                    anything, so I pinch each cheek,
searching, prodding, stretching wet lining,
                    finding at last their secret clasps.
Bone clamps that held his smile intact.
                    Valves clack. Joints lock. Boughs lick the glass
like a gash in the house. His face
                    gapes against my hands—this kind man
who made me—but I can't help. Vents hiss
                    vapor, as I bend to whisper,
"Sorry, so sorry, Dad, I'm so damn sorry."
                    Outside, dark folds and night maws wide.
Pine sap sets to amber.

Rabbit's Foot

Bought for a buck from a curio shop,
the paw was sleek, dyed pink, an amulet
                of bone and hope. Hacked below the hock,
                the trinket fit your palm, burrowed warrens

into pockets. You stroked it. Caressed it. Pressed
delicate cartilage between thumb and finger,
                never stopping to consider the chop.
                Ligament rip, gristle and split, joint-deep pop.

Nor did you imagine amputees—
Peter or Thumper, Bugs or Babs—their hind legs
                pegs, *hippity-stomp*. You didn't think
                of secret thickets, brambles where shadows huddled

and twitched, munched radish, sweet grass, cabbage.
The claw was not a claw to you,
                just a juju, sawed from dewlap and hop.
                Fur talon, talisman of whisker and briar,

at Show & Tell, you held it aloft,
watched eyes go soft with awe. Hand to hand, the foot
                passed clasps, but teacher said, "No hoodoo,"
                returned it warmed to you. You who knew better

than to wonder about witchery—
that thatch at midnight, its moonlit hatchet.
                Best not question protection, a charm's
                inception, the dumb violence of luck.

Random Attack Caught on Camera

"I watch, refresh, watch, refresh. Still, you know, it don't make sense."
—YouTube viewer comment

The clip stutter-starts—jars—then plays
back, black and white and one more time:
same surveillance tape filmed at day-

break, some bridgescape (could be Brooklyn,
London, the Golden Gate). Static
scrims across traffic. Trucks, cabs, vans,

pedestrians. Nothing happens
for seconds—maybe eight—nothing
unmundane, not until a man runs

into the frame, then what happens
won't stop happening. Again
and again, the tape replays. Same

scene, same dawn on screen, its rush-
hour, motor-hum, runner. A woman
enters, walks toward the man

who jogs toward her. Neither turns,
nor pauses to note the other,
but as she passes, he reaches

out. He pushes her over. Over
and over, he pushes her
over, shoves her onto the road. Blurred

at first, the footage loops, recurs
as if rehearsed: mid-footpath,
mid-forties, the jogger approaches,

lopes into focus, appears
never to notice the woman.
Tall, brisk—chosen—she strides toward him,

toward that moment when she lies broken-
doll-splayed in the right-hand lane.
When all that paves the way for her

sensible shoes is sky. The clip
falter-skips—jerks—then plays
back, black and white and one more time.

Spontaneous Human Combustion

"He burned from the inside out, not the outside in. Now that's real proof that this phenomenon's for real. And we're all at risk!"
 —Rick Barton (Director of the International ParaScience Center)

Maybe it begins as a singe, cinders
   hissing from within, kindling beneath skin.
      The flush must feel much like lust at first,

   flicker-licks rippling concentric.
   Or perhaps heat sulks in like a child-
hood fever, caul-wrapping bonnets of fire.

Post-mortem pictures all depict the same
   grim room: its filth and fifth of gin, its Pall
      Mall pack—one smoke left—curtains pulled

   tight against noon. Even in photos, the reek
   seeps through. Yellow on the window's
sill, char-sweet on the carpet in plumes.

Every easy chair can be a pyre. No
   matter, that our bodies are bodies
      of water. Forget the bottles of rot-

   gut, the acetone build-up. Those barbiturates
   and lit cigs blitzing housedresses.
These flare-ups are spontaneous—impetuous

as all of us—bound for ash and about to burst.

Visit to the Phrenologist

Picture the scalp as a mitten
   knit from skin, pulled thin over skull
ridge and dip, over the bulged fist
   of the brain. Do have a seat. Sit.
        Tilt back a bit—there—that's it. This spot
           on the tip-top—here—where the crown
        pocks, curves in two grooves down, where bone
           fused with bone before you were born:
that's the nerve center for wonder.
   Yours rucks. It pits, divots cobble-
stone ruts. Just below swells the hope
   zone, the hub of all want. Small taps
        now, as I inspect that dent
           above your neck, its tender bend
       of nape. Imagine this region's
           an island's little inlet, a cove
cragged by snagcliff and wave: your harbor
   for reason. Our tendencies, you see,
no longer live in the spleen. Or heart.
   Or liver. Hold still, please. I feel
        what can only be crimping, dimpling
           along your coitabellic lobe.
        Which means intimacy hasn't come
           easily, no? Lean into me—
there—just so. Press against my pressing, yes—
   here—this cleft next to your left ear:
that's where memories harden, quartz,
   become dream. Our domes are geodes,
        you know. Rubble crusted around crystal,
           all mud and shine and vug and time,
       formed from the drip-drop of thought,
           eons on eons on iron.

We are rockery, see? Legacies
 of planetary debris, knocked
free from some orb to spin and spin—broken,
 bumped, molten—back again, toward our own core.

Cleaning Out My Father's Closet

All his socks have been tossed. His slacks
boxed, pockets checked for dimes, lint, To-Do
   lists. Soon there will be nothing left
   to find. Mothballs. A pill bottle.
On tip-toe, I move my broom
across the top shelf, whisking
   with the scratch claws make against walls.
   Brisk. Abrading. A sound that can't get out.
Reaching higher, I sweep deeper
and deeper, stretching over the ledge
   where plaster coughs. Rasps. Air can't catch
   its breath. I jab at black, poke
shadow—and goddamn—a softness
nudges back. Two prods, and the object's
   launched: a blur of dun fur, flung over-
   head. But before my mind can form
the word   ANIMAL   this rodent,
or weasel, or ferret hits wallboard
   with a *thumph*, falls floorward to play
   dead. No room to run, so I shoo-
shoo the critter with my broom.
Squirrel-size, it quivers a little
   under the bristles. Then—somehow—
   I know. Swaying, I let go
of the broomstick to pick up my father's
toupee. Mottled beige and silver
   and gray, it weighs what a bunny
   hide might weigh. The underbelly
has clips with tiny hinges, a mesh-net
that itches. I lift his wig and sniff,
   huffing in what's left of him: bits
   of grit, and the scent of months pent up.
Next, I try it on. Yet dad's hair

hat doesn't fit. It slips
   to one side, tickling fringe
     over my eyes, sticking in their trickling.
Few people knew his whorls weren't real.
Till caregivers couldn't give the care
   fake curls required. I stroke their fibers,
     wonder how dignity can be fleeced, again
and again. How "skinned" has opposite meanings.
Back to the top shelf, I return his pelt.

Untitled, Acrylic on Canvas, by Rani (Asian Elephant, Age 30)

The placard assures, she chose this
   blue. She chose blue—a hue somewhere
between dawn cerulean and dusk's
   last azure—because, it tells us,
her species is crepuscular.

Blots smudge—splotch as if dropped—blur
   a foreground that looks far, far off.
But there's contour toward the center.
   Meaning in shape, what the eye tries
to make. The placard says one-point

perspective breaks here. Here, where paint
   thins to a tinge, where a figure
appears. And if not a figure,
   then a form, and if not a form,
then some trace of a frame within

the frame, carving subject from space.
   Nearby, palette knife must have replaced
brush. Blue strokes bruise under hand-
   smack red. Did the tools trainers gave her
become extensions of trunk?

Could that blotch of crimson be sun?
   The placard mentions elephant
intelligence, the influence
   of Expressionism, asks us to view back-
ground slash marks as cranes. But that long,

long line—it's not her horizon—splayed flat. Broken.

Animals in Outer Space

"It's a wonder—with all we've done to other creatures—they don't use our foibles and our own cruel tools to quit us."
—Kelly Asterson, *The Exodus of Species*

A sheep, a duck, and a rooster
went up first. Cupped by a bucket,
strapped all together in a sack-

cloth balloon, they flew. Rose higher—
then higher still—over Versailles,
over Louis, his pale-necked Marie,

till chalk dust wigs were just puffs
off cottonwood trees, topiary
inch-thin twists in a child's labyrinth.

Centuries since: lab rats, fish, rabbits,
cats—then all those wise-eyed
monkeys—have been blasted

past stratosphere. Outside Moscow,
Muttnik sits now (*good puppy*).
Cast in brass, because her coat (combed

soft for photo-ops, publicity
shots with cosmonauts), got cooked
mid-orbit. Next to be launched,

Mexican jumping beans (moth
larvae leap-leaping in seed pods
through stars). Soon after, Madagascar

hissing roaches. Bees and spiders,
lizards and nematodes. Ants

and forty tiny, hearty, come-hell-

or-high-water tardigrades. A bat,
later seen clasped—wings-flat—to space
shuttle *Discovery*, stayed there

unflapped on the fuel tank, as it shrank
out of sight, out of sky. Perhaps
he wanted to join them. The Red Admiral

caterpillars, gerbils, shrimp, newts,
chimps, and gnats. Maybe he went
where they went. No plans to fly back.

Aubade for a Dead Lover

"Clasping wing to wing, foot to foot, swallows dive down to the lake bottom—
sleeping the whole winter underwater."
                  —John Laird, *Aquatic Hibernation*
                  & Suspended Animation in Birds, 1904

This lake is abyssal, carved out by glacier,
laced at the edges with ice. It slices

basalt and sagebrush, catches runoff, glints
through cobalt hills and a town quaint enough

to retain your touch. They say swallows wintered
here once. Before all the yachts, lilypad docks.

Though few watched them drop, it's said that the birds
looked staccato. Just dots overhead. Beads

without thread. Then, a linking—beak hooking
beak, hooking tail-spangle and talon.

To the kid skipping flats at the lakeline,
their plunge must have splashed too fast to catch.

Yet from the bungalow far off—the one
with wind-stitched curtains, three persimmons

on the sill—the fall might have seemed wistful,
their string of wings mystical, a sign

on the window. But for carp circling
and circling through dark, the birds were blue stars

dying, streaking through a sky creased by tide.
Winter stilled the swallows there. Tucked their quills

into nests of silt, till thaw brought lake swell,
hulls, the snag-drag of nets. Up and up, bird

after bird was pulled, each entwined in muckreed
and line. It's told that fishermen brought them

home, revived their flightlust beside stove fires.
Now it's spring again, Love. Numb as you've been—rise.

Terminal Velocity

> —*Artist Julijonas Urbonas created a scale-model rollercoaster designed to euthanize its passengers. With a 1700 ft. "death-drop," the ride would rush blood from the brain, causing a sense of intense euphoria, followed by cerebral hypoxia.*

There is a fair where the dying
    go. A carnival for the frail,
        the ailing, or for those whose day-
            to-day has just gone on too long.
Dusk opens park gates, where neon star-
    dust falls, sifts down on crowds till dawn.
        Under girders, passengers wait
            their turn. Beneath the track's *clack-*
clank-clack, riders line up. Some weep.
    Others wrap arms around bodies
        they've loved. Remembering, they tremble
            with the shudder-bones of trestles.
But the queue keeps moving. It switch-
    backs, single-file, past souvenir
        shacks that hawk photographs, mourning
            plaques—and soon—last breaths are harness-
strapped, belts cinched for ascent, *click-click-*
    gasp. Cables spiral skyward,
        braid like veins—higher, then higher—
            over the metal spine each car climbs
and climbs. It takes two slow minutes
    to reach the top of the death-
        drop. Here, steel glints and gears grind
            against wind. From far off, riders
seem to pause at the apex's crest—teetering
    an in-between—before they scrawl
        a looping script across the moon.
            Before lifting both hands on the brink.

Acknowledgments

Gratitude to the editors of the following publications where these poems first appeared:

3rd Wednesday: "Spontaneous Human Combustion," "Visit to the Phrenologist"

Comstock Review: "Revenants"

Crab Creek Review: "Passage," "View From My Father's Room"

Five Points: "What My Father Couldn't Answer"

Juked: "The Longing of Anatomical Drawings"

The Maine Review: "Terminal Velocity"

North American Review: "Cunnilingus"

PageBoy Magazine: "Bulletin from the Living," "Rabbit's Foot," "Where They Love"

Prairie Schooner: "To Name Is to Own"

RHINO: "Worms"

The Sow's Ear Poetry Review: "Aubade for a Dead Lover"

Under a Warm Green Linden: "Panties Left in a Cemetery"

And endless thanks to Christopher Nelson—for his words offered my way, for his words offered to the world.

About the Poet

Erika Brumett's novel, *Scrap Metal Sky*, was published in 2016 by Shape&Nature Press.